Traditional
HARDANGER
EMBROIDERY

by The Priscilla Publishing Co.

DOVER PUBLICATIONS, INC.
New York

Published in Canada by General Publishing Company, Ltd., 30 Lesmill
Road, Don Mills, Toronto, Ontario.
Published in the United Kingdom by Constable and Company, Ltd.

This Dover edition, first published in 1985, is an unabridged and
unaltered republication of the work first published by The Priscilla Publishing Company, Boston, in 1924 under the title *The Priscilla Hardanger
Book No. 2: A Collection of Typical Norwegian Designs* by Maren Thoresen
and Others. It is reprinted by special arrangement with Coats & Clark,
Inc., P.O. Box 1966, Stamford, Conn. 06904.

Manufactured in the United States of America.
Dover Publications, Inc., 31 East 2nd Street, Mineola, N.Y. 11501.

Library of Congress Cataloging in Publication Data

Priscilla hardanger book no. 2.
  Traditional hardanger embroidery.

  (Dover needlework series)
  Reprint. Originally published: The Priscilla hardanger book no. 2.
Boston, Mass. : Priscilla Pub. Co., c1924.
  1. Hardanger needlework.   I. Priscilla Publishing Company.
II. Title.   III. Series.
TT787.P87   1985   746.44   85-7061
ISBN 0-486-24906-9

Hardanger Embroidery

HARDANGER embroidery takes its name from the district of Hardanger surrounding the fiord of the same name in western Norway. Although usually classified as Norwegian embroidery, the work in its original form is very old, as long ago in Persia and other Asiatic countries it was worked in colored silks on a very fine gauze netting.

The two principal stitches used are satin or kloster stitch for the solid portions of the designs and over and under woven bars for the drawn spaces. These two stitches are varied so as to secure many different decorative effects in combination with eyelets, fagoting and back stitch. The work is easily done and is not trying to the eyes or nerves, but the one absolutely necessary requirement is the correct counting of the threads.

As the square is the principle upon which Hardanger embroidery is based, it is necessary to use a fabric woven with a square mesh, with warp and woof (or filling) threads the same size and counting the same number to the inch, so that when the threads are cut and drawn in both directions the space remaining will be a perfect square. Hardanger canvas, manufactured especially for the purpose, is most commonly used, but various sizes of scrim and Congress canvas are also suitable and many dress materials are adapted to the work.

Two sizes of working threads are necessary, the coarser for the flat embroidery or blocking and the finer for the woven bars. A variety in effect is secured by using a highly mercerized loose-twist cotton (like No. 5 Pearl) for the embroidery and a hard-twist cotton or linen thread for the weaving. Blunt-pointed needles (tapestry needles) are essential, as they separate the threads without splitting them.

The only other necessary item of equipment is a pair of scissors, very sharp and with pointed ends. A dull pair will not cut the canvas clean and close to the embroidery.

Although Hardanger embroidery was originally used by the Norwegian women more especially for the decoration of the apron, which plays such an important part in the national costume, it is readily adapted to various household articles, and because of its formality is especially suited to the living room. The embroidery can be done with thread matching the color of the fabric, but is most effective when there is a color contrast, such as white thread on an écru color canvas and vice versa. Very often, too, a colored thread, like yellow or brown, or any color harmonizing with the color scheme of the room, is used on a white or cream ground, and when the article is a cushion top, a satin lining of corresponding color is added.

When undertaking a piece of Hardanger embroidery the first thing to be done is to deeply overcast the edges of the material to prevent fraying. Many workers like to turn and baste a narrow hem so that the rough ends of the fabric threads will not catch the embroidery cotton.

All kloster stitch work must be done before any threads are cut. It is a very easy matter to make a mistake in counting when laying stitches in kloster stitch figures, and if the threads inside the blocks are cut before the skeleton or framework of the design has been completed, it is practically impossible to correct the error. Another point to remember is that threads are cut along the *ends* of groups of stitches and not along the sides.

The ends of the working cotton should be fastened off neatly. Avoid knots. Start a thread by running it into the canvas which is to be covered and fasten it off by running it back under work already done.

Frontispiece All-Over

ALL-OVER designs are desirable for cushion covers, for utility bags, table pieces, or any article for which a decorative fabric is desired. They are most effective when the design is done in a contrasting color to the background. White on écru is always harmonious.

It is not so difficult to build this design as it might appear. The intersecting lines of kloster blocks constitute the framework. They are worked first, then the star motifs are worked in the spaces between them.

Count forty threads in from both sides of a corner and make an eyelet covering a square of twelve threads. From each corner of the eyelet work a square of two kloster blocks on each side, enclosing twelve threads each way. Cut and draw threads as in Fig. 10 and make picoted woven bars as in Fig. 14. Then out from the four

squares diagonally in each direction make three kloster blocks with eyelets (Fig. 5), then again the squares with woven picot bars and so continue until the material is covered.

Now work the star figures in the spaces between these diagonal lines. Find the centre of a space and make an eight-pointed star, taking the first stitch of each section over two threads and increasing one thread to each stitch until twelve are covered, then decrease one thread in each stitch back to two. There should be a square of four threads uncovered in the centre of this figure. From the centre of each side of the star make a line of seventeen stitches over two threads, each ending in a pointed figure or arrowhead, and finish by enclosing the entire figure with a double line of back stitching in the same thread as used to weave the bars.

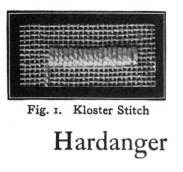

Fig. 1. Kloster Stitch

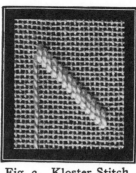

Fig. 2. Kloster Stitch
Worked Diagonally

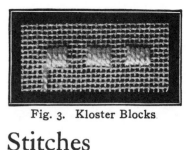

Fig. 3. Kloster Blocks

Hardanger Stitches

Kloster Stitch. The kloster stitches are always worked before any of the cutting of the canvas is attempted. These stitches in their simplest form (Fig. 1) are worked in parallel rows. The thread is brought up through the selected mesh and carried in a straight line over four warp threads, down through the mesh including them, and up through the first mesh to the left of the starting-point. These stitches may be continued in an unbroken straight line, as shown in Fig. 1. If worked on the diagonal of the canvas, each stitch is lifted one mesh, as in Fig. 2.

Kloster Blocks. The little kloster blocks, so typical of Hardanger embroidery and which in some form make the outlines of all the openwork, consist of five stitches over four threads with four warp threads between the blocks (Fig. 3).

To obtain the square or battlemented effect (Fig. 4), a block is worked lengthways of the canvas, and at the completion of the fifth stitch the needle is brought up in the same line, but four meshes to the left. The thread is drawn through, and the needle again inserted in the upper mesh of the last stitch. This makes the first stitch of the second block, widthways of the canvas. The other four stitches are worked and the thread carried down the underside of the work between stitches and canvas to the line of the lower edge of the first block and four meshes to the left. From this point the third block (in line with the first) is begun. When all the horizontal blocks with their alternating uprights have been worked, a second row parallel with the first and connecting with the uprights is worked. The enclosed squares of canvas may be cut out (Fig. 4), or an eyelet may be worked in the centre (Fig. 5).

Diagonal Blocks. Figure 6 shows simple blocking on the diagonal of the canvas. After making the last stitch of the horizontal block bring the needle up on a line with top of block but four meshes to left. After making fifth stitch of this block, bring needle up in same mesh as bottom of last stitch.

Double Diagonal Blocks. Figure 7 shows a double row of Fig. 6, worked so as to enclose square of canvas counting four threads in each direction.

Mitred Kloster Stitch Corners. The mitred corner (Fig. 8) is very attractive, and in some places may be used with excellent effect; but it is not good for a buttonholed border, as the last or corner stitches are over only one or two warp threads, and when the outside canvas is cut away, the cut ends under the corner stitches will pull out. If mitred corners are desired for a border the canvas underneath should be reenforced with a strip of soft lawn through which the buttonholing is worked with each stitch into the canvas. When the border is completed, the uncovered portions of the lawn are cut away. The buttonholed border may be still further strengthened by a line of machine stitching close to the outer edge of the stitches. A very pretty result is produced by working a second row of close buttonhole-stitches just over the edge of the first row after the outer canvas has been cut away.

Diagonal Buttonholing for Edge. The edge of Hardanger embroidery is usually finished with a hem-stitched hem or a row of close buttonhole-stitches over four threads. At each rounding of a corner the stitches are taken in the corner mesh and carried along diagonally until four warp threads are covered. The direction is then turned at right angles and the buttonhole-stitches worked still from the same mesh until the corner is turned. They are then continued until an

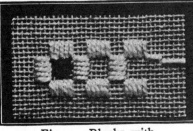

Fig. 4. Blocks with
Cut Canvas

Fig. 5. Blocks with
Eyelet

Fig. 6. Diagonal Blocks

4

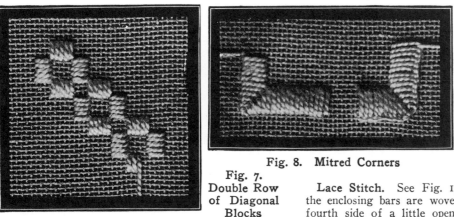

Fig. 8. Mitred Corners

Fig. 7.
Double Row
of Diagonal
Blocks

long enclosing a square of sixteen warp threads with four threads cut and drawn at each corner, leaving a group of eight threads at the middle of each side. These are divided into pairs of four each, and woven in the usual way. It is an effective way to fill a large figure.

inner corner is reached. Here they are parted at right angles. Figure 9 shows this buttonholed edge worked outside a line of diagonal blocks.

Cutting Threads. Great care must always be exercised in cutting and drawing fabric threads for the openwork portions of Hardanger designs, and this part of the work should never be done until the kloster stitch figures have been completed and found to be correct. This is especially important in working a border around a square. A mistake made in laying kloster stitches can easily be rectified, but a fabric thread once cut and drawn cannot be replaced.

Fabric threads should always be cut along the ends of kloster stitches and never along their sides. In other words the cut threads always extend in the same direction as the stitches of the adjoining blocks. Figure 10 shows very clearly what is meant by this.

Weaving Bars. Figure 11 shows the method of weaving the groups of four warp threads left after the cut threads have been drawn out. The needle is passed under the first two threads, up at the middle, and over the last two threads. These bars should be woven closely and evenly with a much finer thread.

To Weave Double Bars. A pleasing variation of a kloster stitch figure is shown in Fig. 12, each side of which consists of a kloster block seventeen stitches

Lace Stitch. See Fig. 13. In making this stitch the enclosing bars are woven until the middle of the fourth side of a little open square is completed. A single buttonhole-stitch is then worked into the middle of each of the other three sides, the thread returned to the fourth side, and the remaining half bar woven (see also Fig. 18).

The outline of Fig. 13 is formed by diagonal blocks, each arm consisting of a square finished on the fourth side by a woven bar.

Picoted Woven Bars. A new arrangement of kloster stitches is shown in Fig. 14. Each side consists of two triangles meeting at the middle. The first or end stitch is over eight threads. The succeeding ones are over seven, six, five, four, three, and two threads. The other half is then increased by working over three, four, five, six, seven, and eight threads. After the four corner threads are cut and drawn, the remaining bars are closely woven and decorated with French-knot picots (Fig. 14). The needle is passed under two threads as usual, and while in this position the thread is brought forward and around the needle two or three times. The needle is pulled through and

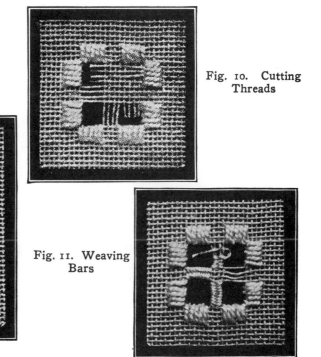

Fig. 10. Cutting Threads

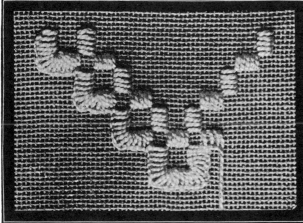

Fig. 9. Diagonal Buttonholing for Edge

Fig. 11. Weaving Bars

Fig. 12. Weaving Double Bars

Fig. 13. Way of Working Lace Stitch

continued until the second bar is completed. The thread is carried along the blocking to the third bar, which is woven for half its length. The thread is then carried three times back and forth between this and the second bar, the connection closely buttonholed, and the third bar completed. When the fourth bar is woven half its length, the three connecting threads are carried to the third bar and buttonholed. Then three are carried to the first bar and buttonholed, completing the circle. The weaving of the fourth bar is then completed.

Eyelets. The eyelets shown in Fig. 17 are made with the finer thread. A square of four threads is included in each of the small eyelets. The needle is brought up at the corner mesh of this square, and from the middle mesh a close over-and-over stitch is taken into each mesh along the four sides of the square. No fabric threads are cut, but drawing each stitch tight pulls them away from the centre and makes the opening. Six and eight threads are included in the larger eyelets.

An eyelet is frequently used to fill the centre of a kloster stitch block (see Fig. 5).

Double Bars with Lace Stitch (see Fig. 18). Each side of this square is enclosed with a continuous row of stitches, four over four threads, four over eight, five over twelve, four over eight, and four over four, enclosing a square twenty threads each way. Eight threads are cut away at the corners in each direction, leaving four threads in the middle of each side. These are divided into groups of two, and are closely woven with the finer thread over one and under one. The first bar is woven for its entire length. When the second bar is half woven, the thread is entered in a buttonhole-stitch into the middle of the woven bar, then into the adjoining side, then into the next side and back to the half-woven bar, which is then completed. These

the thread drawn up tightly as before, and is again passed under the same two threads to keep the picot in position at the outer edge of the bar. It is then passed under the other two threads and a second picot made on the other side of the bar, the weaving of which is then continued.

Twisted Bars. To make the frame for the twisted bars shown in process in Fig. 15 a square of canvas twelve threads each way is enclosed on each side by a block of four stitches over four threads, five over eight threads, and four over four threads. The four corner threads of the enclosed square are cut and drawn out. The remaining bars are closely woven over two and under two threads. At the completion of each bar the thread is carried from the centre diagonally across to the outside corner of the adjoining little square and twisted back. If preferred, these twisted bars may be two long bars reaching from opposite corners of the enclosed squares and crossing in the middle.

This motif has been used many times in forming the more elaborate designs shown in the back of this book.

Buttonholed Circle. Figure 16. In this detail the four corner threads each way of the enclosed square of twelve threads are cut and drawn out. The remaining groups of four threads each are then woven and embellished with a buttonholed circle. The first group of four threads is woven over two and under two for its entire length. The weaving of the second bar is begun at the centre of the square and woven over two and under two for half its length. The thread is then entered into the middle of the first, or completed, bar, back to the second bar, and again into the first. This makes three threads connecting the two bars. These are closely buttonholed back to the second bar and the weaving

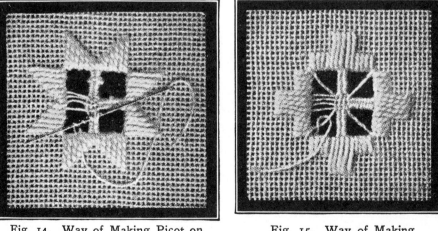

Fig. 14. Way of Making Picot on Woven Bar

Fig. 15. Way of Making Twisted Bars

6

buttonhole-stitches are drawn tight enough to pull the bars out of line and leave an oval opening between the pairs. The other three corners are filled in the same way.

Fagoting Stitch. Figure 20 shows a band of four rows of fagoting. The fagot-stitch is simply a binding together of two fabric threads, from the same mesh, first lengthways, and then widthways of the canvas. The needle is entered from the under side of the canvas at 1 (see Fig. 19), entered into 2, and up again at 1. The thread is drawn tightly, and the needle again entered into 2,

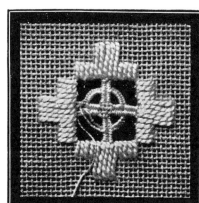

Fig. 16. Buttonholed Circle

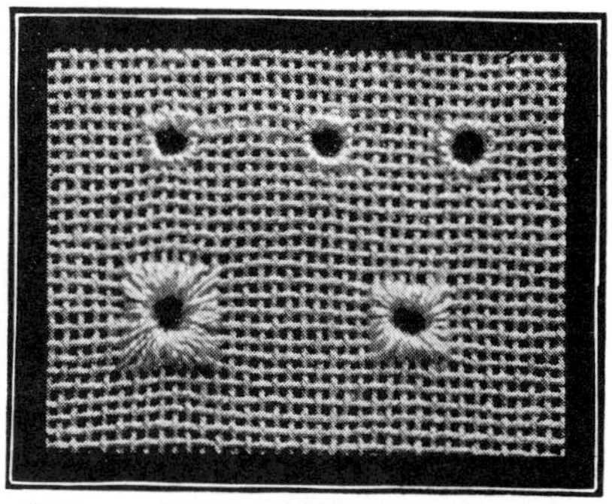

and up again at 3 two threads to the left of 1. From here a stitch into 1 and out at 3 is made and the thread drawn tightly. The needle is again entered into 1 and brought up two threads below 3 at 4. The next stitch is from 3 to 4. The next is from 3 to 5, two threads to the left of 4. Then from 5 back to 4, and out at 5. The next is from 4 diagonally across two threads to 6. The work is so continued across the space, completing the first row of fagoting. In the second row the needle is brought up into 2 of the first row, entered two threads above and out again at 2, and the work continued as in the first row. In this way the required number of rows are made one at a time. This stitch sounds much more complicated than it really is, and it may be accomplished with great ease and speed. The worker soon discovers that it is really a binding tightly together of two fabric threads, each pair at right angles to its predecessor and continuing in a zigzag line diagonally across the canvas.

With a knowledge of the stitches here given, the needle-worker need not hesitate to undertake any

Fig. 17. Way of Working Eyelets

design in Hardanger embroidery, but always the counting of the threads must be exactly accurate. To the inventive worker many new combinations will present themselves. Stitches may be varied, combined, or added to, until beautiful new results are obtained. A sampler upon which to practise these stitches and retain them for future use is almost imperative.

The worked pieces which follow are merely suggestive of the many interesting combinations which are possible. The embroidered frame which decorates the cover makes use of the square Hardanger eyelet to border the edges of rectangular spaces, which are filled with parallel bars woven on four fabric threads and the spaces between the woven bars crossed diagonally in both directions with twisted bars. It is an unusual combination which does not appear on any of the finished pieces illustrated, yet would make a very nice border for a luncheon set. Fagoting, kloster stitch, and picoted woven bars are other stitches which have been used on the cover embroidery.

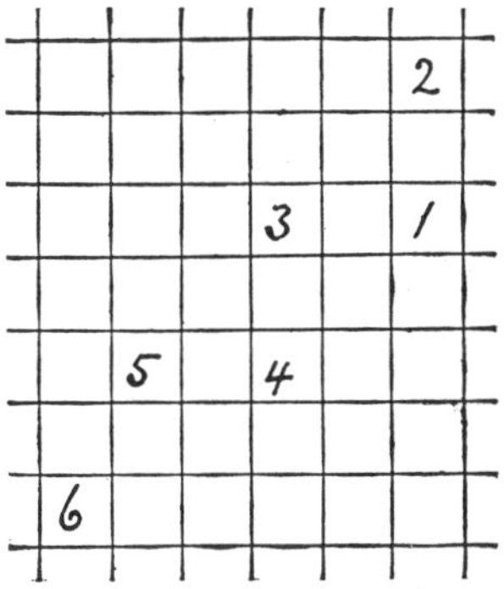

Fig. 19. Diagram for Working Fagot Stitch. See Fig. 20

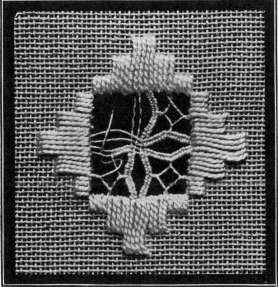

Fig. 18. Double Bars with Lace Stitch

Fig. 20. Way of Working Fagot Stitch. See Diagram, Fig. 19

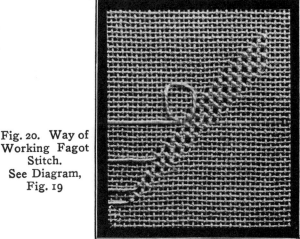

Simple Borders

BORDERS in Hardanger are a delightful decoration for table runners, chair backs, curtains, tea cloths, doilies, and bags. The designs which follow have been chosen because they are simple and will not take long to execute.

Border No. 1 is done in plain and diagonal kloster blocks with a background of plain and picoted woven bars. It is a good border for table squares, runners, or curtains. Worked on material counting eighteen threads to the inch it measures about two inches in width. Allow sufficient material for hem, and work a row of kloster blocks for outer edge of border. There must be six blocks to each repeat of the border unit plus one for each corner. When working a border for a square this outer row of blocks should be accurately placed all around, turning corners as shown in detail. Count twenty-eight threads in from outer row and work second row of blocks for inner edge of border, placing them directly above blocks forming outer border. Now work double row of diagonal blocks (Fig. 7) from outer to inner corner and then back and forth from edge to edge of border. Cut and draw groups of four threads from the triangular spaces between the

diagonal rows of kloster blocks and weave bars on the groups of threads remaining, decorating the bars in the spaces along the outer edge with picots (Fig. 14).

Scalloped Edge No. 2 also uses kloster blocks and woven bars and adds eyelets (Fig. 17), fagoting (Fig. 19), star stitch and diagonal buttonholing (Fig. 9) for the edge. The row of cut kloster blocks (Fig. 4) which outlines the top of this border, is worked first, then the scalloped edge, and last of all the patterns in the points. Remembering that kloster stitch blocks are done in multiples of four it is easy to count the threads in the pattern, forty-eight between the bottom of the row of cut kloster blocks and the buttonholed edge. Allow an additional inch or more on the edge for convenience in handling.

Having worked the row of cut kloster blocks, count down twelve threads from the bottom of the first block and start the diagonal kloster blocks for the inner edge of the scallops, seven steps down and then up. Next do the diagonal buttonholing, but do not cut away the edge until the patterns in the scallops are worked. You can use the open and closed patterns alternately as pictured or one style only. Count four threads below cut kloster blocks and work the upper row of kloster stitch (solid or blocked according to the pattern) directly over each point. The rest of the figure will then easily follow. There should be thirty-six stitches in the solid row. The eyelet is worked over eight threads. Each section of the pointed figure above it is worked gradually over two to eight threads and then back again to two, increasing on one side of a section and decreasing on the other. The stitches in the side points are vertical, those forming the bottom points are horizontal. As one section joins another the stitches up to the widest part are taken into the same meshes as those in the section preceding. The first stitch in each side section is taken vertically

Border No. 1. A Simple Border, Easy to Execute, Suitable for Curtains, Tea Cloths, Table Runners or Bags

8

tinue both outer and inner borders in the proper direction.

Border No. 3 is made up of kloster stitch squares with open centres and square eyelets. Begin with a solid row of kloster stitches over four threads. Then work the squares (Fig. 15), planning so that the longest stitches come four threads from the band of kloster stitches. Leave four threads between figures of first row and work squares of second row so that the end stitches of the various blocks will fall in the same meshes with those of first row. The threads in the centre of each square are cut and drawn so as to leave groups of four in the centre. These are woven with picots (Fig. 14) and the spaces filled with twisted bars.

The square eyelets are worked over eight threads according to the method described on page 7 (Fig. 17) and should be placed so that they come exactly between the large figures and in the same line of meshes as the outer stitches. To turn a corner work a large figure in place of the eyelet at upper right and extend the border from it. When turning a corner

over two threads and into the same mesh with the first and last stitches of the kloster block. The first stitch of each bottom section is taken horizontally over two threads and into the same mesh with its neighbor on either side.

In the alternate points work the diagonal blocks and woven bars, then the double line of back stitches, each taken over two threads.

To turn a corner with this pattern first work a second open figure in an upright position to the right of the first with the inner edge of the kloster stitch band taken into the same line of meshes as the end stitch of the first figure. Having done this it will be an easy matter to con-

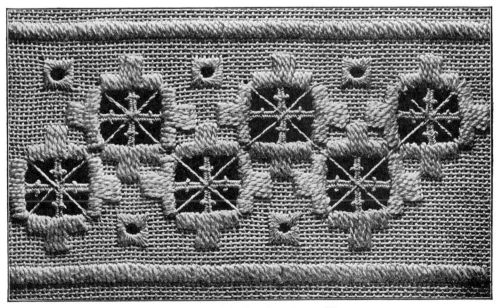

Border No. 3 is Good to Top a Hem

the solid rows of kloster stitches should be mitered as in Fig. 8.

Border No. 4 shows how effective an exceedingly simple pattern can be when applied to a tea cloth. Kloster blocks and plain and picoted woven bars are the only stitches used. The material is 45-inch mercerized Hardanger cloth. No. 5 Pearl cotton is used for the kloster stitches.

Start the work about two inches from the edge of the cloth to allow for hem. Begin with outer row of corner kloster blocks and work in both directions. There should be three blocks for the base of each figure and two between. Twelve threads inside lay a second row of blocks, making sure that they fall directly above the stitches in the outer row. Leave four threads and work another row. Again leave twelve threads and

work row of blocks for inner edge of border. Now lay diagonal blocks connecting the straight lines. This completes the skeleton of the pattern. To prepare the material for the woven bars alternately cut and draw and leave four threads between the double row of blocks through the centre and inside the triangular motifs.

If desired, the border can be repeated to form a small square in the centre of the cloth. Make sure that the motifs fall exactly over those in the border by running in a dark thread as a guide. The illustration shows a little less than a quarter of the cloth. You can make this centre ornament any size you choose, having an odd number of motifs on each side if there is an odd number in the border. Measure in from the centre on each side and plan accordingly.

This border is so very simple to handle that it

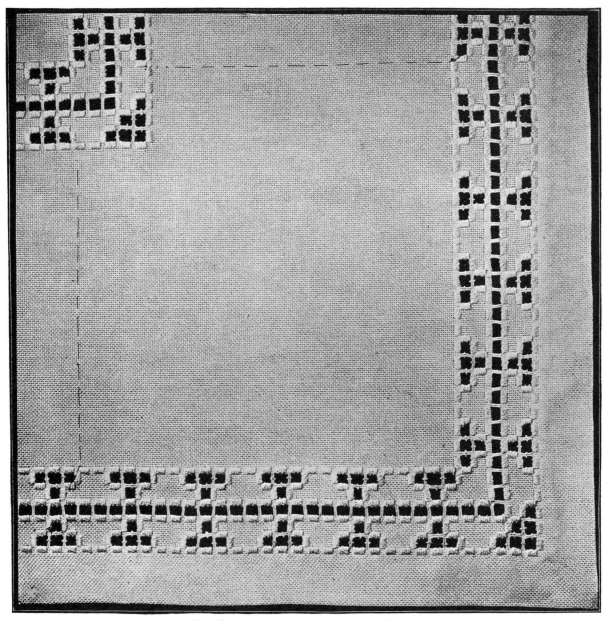

Tea Cloth Decorated with Border No. 4

Border No. 4. This Detail Shows How Easy it is
to Turn a Corner

might be used to decorate scrim curtains without involving a great deal of work. When completed the hem should be turned and fastened invisibly along the outer row of blocks.

Border No. 5, shown below, is particularly good for utility bags and makes a nice decoration for the ends of oblong pillows. This pattern is begun by working the square figures in the centre, and then the pointed edge is added on either side. Fifty-six threads must be allowed, plus whatever width hem is desired. Find the centre of the space where it is desired to lay the border and make the squares, thirteen stitches over four threads on four sides, taking the end stitch of each side into the same mesh with the end stitch of the adjoining side, but in the opposite direction. Make as many squares as needed for the length of the border, leaving eight threads between them. Leave four threads on either side and make the pointed bands. Take the first stitch over four threads in the same line of meshes into which fall the stitches of the side of the square below. In each succeeding stitch take one thread more until the 11th is over fourteen threads (the middle of the square), then decrease to four threads. Make seven more stitches over four threads; then commence next point. There are twenty-one stitches in each pyramid.

Finish the centres of the squares before cutting and drawing the background for the woven bar filling. The square eyelets which fill each alternating figure are worked over six threads each.

The threads inside the other square figures are cut and drawn in both directions, leaving a group of four threads at the centre of each side for the picoted woven bars, to be worked as shown in Fig. 14. Then the twisted bars are laid as in Fig. 15. Now cut and draw the fabric threads surrounding these square figures, leaving groups of four for the woven bars as pictured.

Border No. 5 is Very Open and Lacy

Chair Back or Table Runner

THE repeating units which frame this border are easy to do and adaptable to a variety of purposes. Two will make an end for a narrow table runner, three is a good number for a chair back or wider runner, and for a davenport back the number can be increased at will.

Allowing about an inch for margin, count in eight threads from side, thirty-two up from bottom and lay frame of kloster stitch block for first open figure — seven blocks for base, ten for length of each arm and two for width. Start diagonal blocks for inner edge of point between first and second base blocks. Work six blocks down and five up.

Leave twenty-eight threads and make next figure in same way.

Start between first and second kloster blocks on sides at corners for border, working three sides of square to top of figure and then four sides as in Fig. 4.

Turn hem on sides to outer row of blocks and you are ready to buttonhole scalloped edge. Working over same four threads as used for first kloster block in border buttonhole end of hem, then work diagonally five scallops down and four up joining the diagonal lines of kloster blocks. Work twenty-nine stitches over four threads between figures and continue around next point, four scallops down and four up, and so on.

Cut and draw four threads in each direction inside blocks forming large figures, leaving four threads between for weaving. The main bar through the centre is picoted, the side bars are plain.

In the plain spaces between the openwork figures make three rows of kloster blocks directly above the straight buttonholed edge and put an eyelet in the centre of each. In the space above make three blocks with cut centres and between the arms of each open figure work a kloster stitch figure.

Detail A.
Section Chair
Back on
Page 13

Chair Back or
Table Runner.
Detail on
Page 12

Table Runner.
Detail and De-
scription on
Page 14

Detail B. Section of Runner Shown on Page 13. Ecru Hardanger Cloth Worked with
White Mercerized Cotton

This **Table Runner,** made of mercerized Hardanger cloth counting sixteen threads to the inch, when finished will measure about fifteen inches in width. Allow about four inches for hems. Beginning work at corner count twelve threads in from hem on both sides and bottom, make six kloster stitch blocks in both directions and join with a line of diagonal blocks. Next make the three squares (Fig. 15) meeting the inner edge of the triangular figure, filling the space inside the squares with fagoting stitch (Figs. 19 and 20). On the end parallel with the top and bottom of the last square make rows of kloster stitches, four over four threads, thirteen over eight threads, then four over four threads again. The next square is exactly like that in the corner and is the centre of the end.

Start the large open figure by working eight diagonal blocks along the inner edge of the three corner squares, then fifteen diagonal blocks upward toward the centre and the same number down again to the opposite corner. The arrangement of the blocks which form the lower edge of the open figure is clearly shown in the detail above, the square eyelet over eight threads coming directly in the centre. This detail also shows the arrangement of squares with fagot stitch centres and small connecting figures to form borders along the sides. Four lines of back stitches border the top of the large open motif, the two middle lines being taken into the same meshes.

Figures 11, 13, and 14 show in detail the process of making the woven bar, picot bar, and lace filling stitches.

Butterfly Border

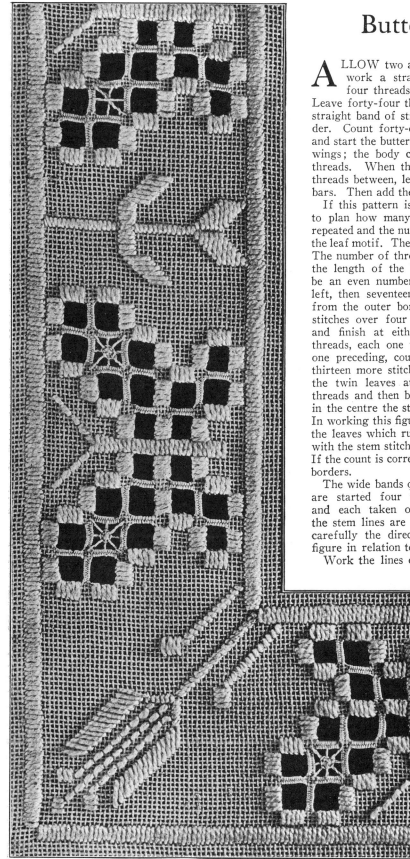

ALLOW two and one-fourth inches for a hem and work a straight band of kloster stitches over four threads in both directions from the corner. Leave forty-four threads inside this and work a second straight band of stitches for the inner edge of the border. Count forty-eight threads from the outer corner and start the butterfly figure. Kloster blocks outline the wings; the body consists of thirty stitches over four threads. When this has been done cut and draw the threads between, leaving groups of four for the woven bars. Then add the spider markings.

If this pattern is to border a square cloth it is well to plan how many times the butterfly motif is to be repeated and the number of threads to be left between for the leaf motif. The butterfly requires sixty-eight threads. The number of threads to be left between depends upon the length of the border between corners, but should be an even number. As pictured, twelve threads are left, then seventeen stitches worked over two threads from the outer border to the first leaf. Make eleven stitches over four threads for the centre of this leaf and finish at either end with six stitches over six threads, each one taken one thread in advance of the one preceding, counting toward the inside. Then do thirteen more stitches for top of stem and finish with the twin leaves at top, working over two to seven threads and then back to two. Where the leaves meet in the centre the stitches are taken into the same holes. In working this figure be careful to place the stitches of the leaves which run in one direction in the same holes with the stem stitches which go in the opposite direction. If the count is correct this figure fits exactly between the borders.

The wide bands of kloster stitch in the corner figures are started four threads in from the outer border and each taken over six threads. The stitches of the stem lines are each taken over two threads. Note carefully the direction of the stitches in this corner figure in relation to the motifs on either side.

Work the lines of back stitch for butterfly antennæ and stamens of corner motifs diagonally over two threads each.

The sample shown in the illustration is so little reduced in size that every stitch and fabric thread can be easily counted.

This Butterfly Border is Easy to do

Curtain Borders

SCRIM curtains can be very beautifully decorated with Hardanger borders. It is a good idea to make the curtains the length and width desired and then to work the border about an inch inside the hem, which should be two inches in width and topped with double hem-stitching about half an inch in width.

Curtain Border No. 1. Start fifteen threads in from the hem at the corner and make nine kloster stitches over four threads, skip four threads and make ten kloster blocks of five stitches each separated by four threads, again

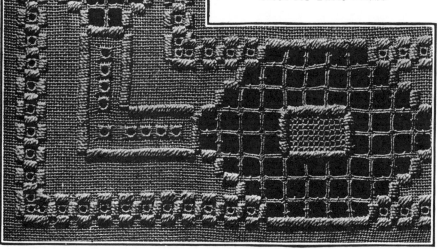

Curtain Border No. 1 is Equally Effective Worked on Hardanger Cloth for Table Pieces

skip four threads and make a
of thirty-seven stitches, which fo
the side of the large openw
figure. At each end of this solid
respectively. For the top of th
six diagonal blocks down to t
parallel with those first made,
line of thirteen stitches and th
The figure in the centre of t
threads in length and thirteen
filled with fagoting stitch (Fig.
threads after cutting and drawing
In either direction from the s
squares with eyelet centres. Th
and seventeen squares worked be
Midway between these two nar
lay solid lines of kloster stitche
figures and in the centre of the
over six threads.

Curtain Border No. 2 is als
kloster blocks (Fig. 3) in bo

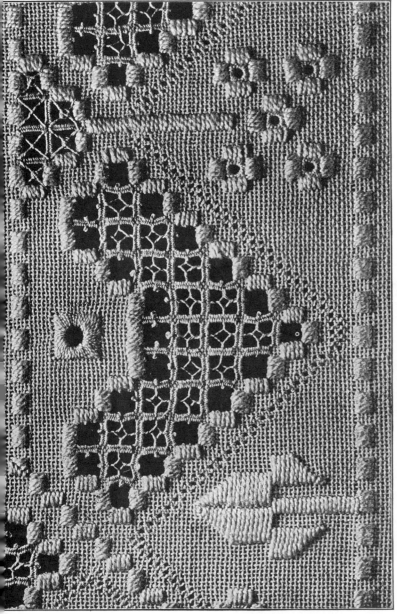

from both sides and make a row of blocks parallel with the first for the inner edge of the border.

For the openwork figure count eight threads from the inside corner and make a line of thirteen stitches, then down toward the centre three diagonal blocks and a line of twenty-one stitches for the centre of the top of the figure. The rest of the frame can easily be counted, and from the illustration can also be seen the placement of the rose tree motif which alternates with the open triangle motif and the two leaf motifs which appear only at the corner. The large eyelets cover twelve threads When all the figures are complete add the line of fagoting stitches.

Curtain Border No. 2 Combines a Variety of Stitches

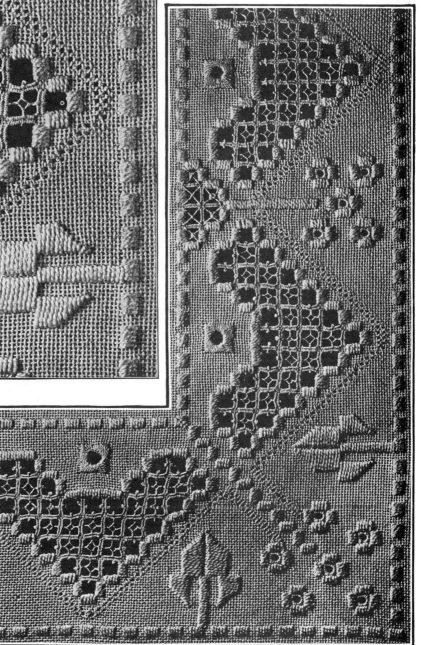

e six diagonal blocks to right and left
nake a line of thirteen stitches, then
side, a line of thirty-seven stitches
al blocks back toward the centre, a
of the first open figure is complete.
ork is twenty-one stitches over four
in width, the space enclosed being
he woven bars are worked on four
rnating threads as in Figs. 10 and 11.
his figure run lines of kloster block
s turned as shown in the illustration
figures along side and bottom.
ecting borders and parallel with them
hreads apart to join the ends of the
tween work connecting eyelets made

from the corner. Make a row of
ons. Count seventy-six threads in

Small Square Tea Cloth

THIS design may be worked out in many varieties of detail, as shown in the two succeeding illustrations of centrepieces on pages 20 and 21.

It is finished with an inch and a quarter hem, and for this and the threads drawn for the hemstitching which tops it, three inches of margin must be allowed. Using material counting not less than seventeen threads to the inch this design can be put upon 36-inch material.

Inside this margin the warp threads are counted one hundred twelve threads up from the front and twenty-four threads in from the side of the canvas. From this point, A, a row of twenty-two diagonal kloster blocks (Fig. 6) is worked across towards the front edge of the canvas. A second row of sixteen more blocks is

worked at right angles in toward the centre of the canvas. At right angles to this row and in the same direction as the first row sixteen more blocks are worked. This brings the work to the middle of one side of the design. To insure accuracy of work it is well to continue around the entire square, returning to the starting-point A, and prove the work by putting in the outer half of each of the large squares (Fig. 15) that follow inside the first row of work. By making these blocks one half at a time the working thread is carried without waste from one block to the next (see Detail C).

Returning again to A the second half of these large squares is worked. Later, when all the kloster stitches

of these squares have been put in the threads of these enclosed squares are cut and drawn out (Fig. 10) and the remaining threads closely woven with the finer cotton (Fig. 11).

This band of large squares is continued entirely around the border and at each corner forms three sides of an enclosed square of the canvas. Three similar large squares (Fig. 15) complete the fourth side. Around the edge of this enclosed square three rows of fagoting (Fig. 19) are worked, and in the centre a large 8-pointed star (Detail D). Each section or diamond is one-eighth of the complete star, and consequently reaches from diameter to diagonal. In each section the cotton is carried over two threads twice, over four twice, over six twice, over eight twice, over ten twice and reduced in the same order. In the centre space of the star an eyelet is worked and in each corner of the square between the points, a group of eight eyelets.

Detail C. Use Diagonal Buttonhole Edge Only When Desired to Complete Pattern at This Point

Inside the border formed by the large squares a single row of diagonal kloster blocks (Fig. 6) is worked, and twenty-eight threads farther in there is a second row of these same blocks. The usual threads in the space between these two rows are cut and drawn out and the remaining threads woven into bars, each decorated with a picot at each side (Fig. 14). An inner row of diagonal kloster blocks (Fig. 7) completes this part of the design.

Between the corner and middle points at the outside of the design a double row of kloster stitches (Fig. 7) is worked in a point enclosing a square eight blocks each way. The canvas within this square is cut and drawn and the remaining threads woven, each bar decorated with two little picots (Fig. 14).

One of the most effective parts of the work is the band of seven rows of fagoting (Fig. 20) that encloses

the entire design. Each little triangle outside this fagoted band is enclosed with a single row of blocks and at the middle of the outer side a half star is worked, each section of which consists of a diamond composed of ten stitches taken over one, two, three, four, five, five, four, three, two, and one threads respectively (Detail E).

Diagonally across the four corners a double row of diagonal blocks is worked and along the other two sides of these corners a single straight row of blocks. In the corner of this space is worked an arrowhead, or one-fourth of a star, and at each side one-half of a star, using the same directions as in the whole stars.

(*Right*) **Detail D**

(*Left*) **Detail E**

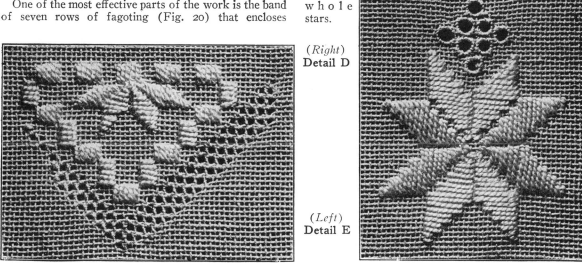

Two Centrepieces of Similar Construction

THIS centrepiece is identical with the square cloth on page 18 in lines of construction, but omits the hem and border decoration and completes the edge with diagonal buttonholing (Fig. 9). Although the stitchery might be identical with the square cover, some slight variations have been made. In the large squares (Fig. 15) which border the various parts of the design twisted bars have been carried diagonally from corners to centre, as in the detail, and enclosing the star figure in each corner there are but three rows of fagoting and five eyelets instead of eight in each group.

It will be noticed also that the count of the blocks forming the structural lines of this piece is not the same as the square on page 18. Worked as illustrated, on canvas counting seventeen threads to the inch, this centrepiece will be fully as large as the square, even though the hem and outer border are omitted.

A very beautiful variation of this same design worked on a very fine piece of mercerized canvas is shown on page 21.

The work is begun at the diagonal of a corner, as in the two preceding, but not less than one hundred forty warp threads up from the front edge and not less than twenty in from the side. A row of thirty diagonal blocks (Fig. 6) is worked across the corner towards the front. The next row, at right angles, is twenty-four

blocks long, as is also the third row, which reaches the middle of the front side of the design. Just inside this row the border of large squares (Fig. 15) is worked — seven squares on each side of the corner square and reaching to the middle of the side. Eyelets are worked between the outer corners of each of these squares entirely around the design. The bars in the drawn centres of each of these large squares are closely woven and decorated with picots (Fig. 14).

Inside the square border of large squares a single row of diagonal blocks (Fig. 6) is worked. A second row of diagonal blocks is worked thirty-six warp threads in, extending from the corners eighteen blocks towards the middle of each side. From this point a line of single blocks (Fig. 3) is worked to meet the first row, and the space enclosed is cut and drawn and filled in with woven bars decorated with picots (Fig. 14) and a line of lace stitch (Fig. 13) worked into the middle squares.

The square of openwork (Fig. 14) in the angle between the middle and corner points is twelve blocks long on each side.

The edge is finished in diagonal buttonhole points with an eyelet in each one.

In the corner squares of canvas enclosed by the border of large kloster blocks three rows of fagoting (Fig. 19) are worked, and in the centre a star. Between the star and each corner of the space is a square group of seventeen eyelets.

Octagon Centrepiece

THIS centrepiece is a very closely decorated octagon measuring about eighteen inches in diameter when worked on fine Congress Canvas or scrim counting twenty-six threads to the inch.

The broad band about midway between the centre and the edge of the design, composed of a row of large squares (Fig. 15) between double rows of diagonal kloster blocks with eyelet centres, as shown in Detail F, page 23, may be considered the keynote of the design and the work begun at one of its corners. This point must be not less than fifty warp threads up from the front edge nor less than two hundred fifty in from the side. Each outside row of this band consists of twenty-five groups of Fig. 7. Work an eyelet inside of these and all other little groups of four kloster blocks in the design. Inside this border and with the outer points worked into the same meshes as the outer ones of the first border work an interrupted border of large squares, Fig. 15. First the corner square and the two squares at either side of it are worked, then two blocks of Fig. 7, followed by two more squares of Fig. 15. Two more squares of Fig. 7 indicate the middle of each side of the border. When this work has been completed on all four sides work a second row of double diagonal blocks entirely around the inside of the square to correspond with the outer edge.

Detail F. Section of Octagon on Page 22

Twenty-eight warp threads in from this band work another row of Fig. 7.

If preferred the centre may be of the canvas without any decoration. As shown it is filled with a design composed of four parts, each one consisting of four squares of Fig. 16, three of which have the three outer sides worked with the kloster stitches (four over four threads, four over eight, five over twelve, four over eight, and four over four), the fourth or inner side of these squares being left unworked. The fourth or centre section of each large square has the kloster stitches on two sides only (see Detail F). Eight threads are cut and drawn in each direction at the corners of all these squares and the remaining threads woven over two and under two threads (Fig. 11). The central squares in each corner and in the middle are filled with the lace stitch (Fig. 13). In the four little open squares formed by the woven bars in each enclosed square, diagonals and diameters are carried across the space, during the weaving, and twisted back. When the last of these threads has been twisted back to the centre they are all tied together and a ribbed wheel worked by carrying the cotton each time around the last bar and under the next one.

The entire outer part of the design now remains to be worked. Beginning six blocks in from each corner work a band of five diagonal groups of Fig. 7 at right angles to the long band toward the edge of the cloth.

A row of Fig. 4 on the straight of the canvas and Fig. 7 on the diagonal is then worked entirely around the design, connecting the diagonal bands. The two outer blocks of the end figure of each band of five and one block of each corner figure of the outer border and of the large square first worked form a part of this row of kloster blocks. The oblongs thus enclosed at each side of the square are divided by two rows of Fig. 7, placed two blocks apart, into two squares with an oblong space between. These squares are decorated with an eight-pointed star, each of the eight sides increased one thread each stitch, over one thread, over two, and so on until ten threads are covered and then decreased in the same way. An eyelet in the centre and one near each corner of the star complete this part of the design.

Twenty-eight threads out from the last border a row of single straight and diagonal kloster blocks is worked parallel with the last row, and a buttonholed border, Fig. 8, on the diagonal and Fig. 9 on the straight sides finishes the edge.

This completes the solid portions of the design and we are now ready to cut and draw the fabric threads in groups of four in all undecorated spaces enclosed by the

(*Continued on page 29*)

Cushion Cover

WORKED on scrim of medium weave this cushion cover will measure about eighteen inches square. The design is novel in combining cross stitch with the kloster stitch and in the introduction of color. All the solid portions of the design are color, the cross stitches and woven bars with their various filling stitches are white.

A quarter section of the design is shown in Detail G, page 25, which is sufficiently clear so that the threads and stitches can be counted. Start the work at a corner and lay a border of parallel kloster stitches over four threads in both directions, mitering the corners. Count thirty-six

threads from the corner and lay a double row of diagonal blocks across from one side to the other. Inside this double row of blocks and starting at the border work a diagonal line of cross stitches, each one over the same four threads covered by a kloster block and worked into the same mesh with the end stitch of the block. Next to the end stitch at top and bottom lay two more cross stitches, the three touching the border. Four more cross stitches, placed diagonally from them and at right angles to the long row, complete the two ends of the oblong space we are building. From these four cross stitches are worked inward and connected

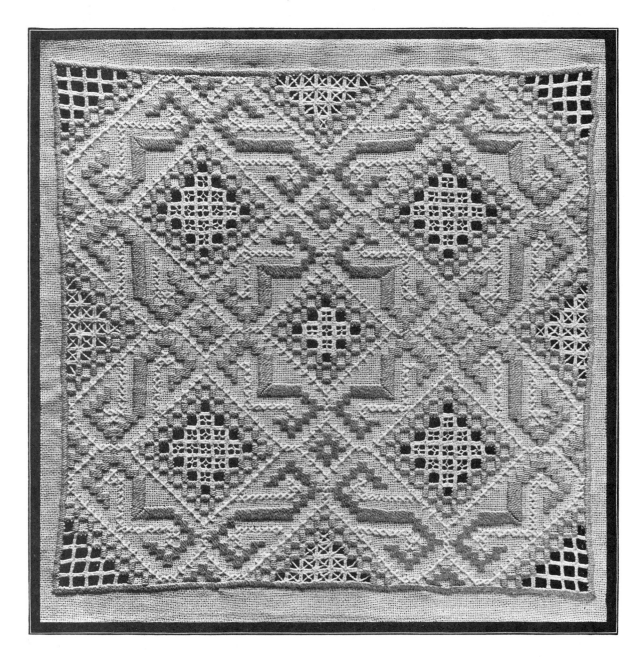

Detail G. Section of Cushion Cover on Page 24

with a row of ten cross stitches parallel with the first long row and completing the outline of the oblong. This row of ten stitches forms one side of a square, which in turn is the base of the four oblongs which surround it. Just inside this cross stitch square work a double row of diagonal kloster stitches and then proceed to lay in the figures inside the oblong spaces.

The centre bar of this figure in the spaces on either side of the corner consists of thirty-one parallel stitches taken over four threads. The placement of this bar and the other stitch groups which form the figure is shown in Detail G. In the corner oblong space and the one directly opposite, the centre of the figure consists of two bars laid at right angles to each other, each having sixteen parallel stitches over eight threads and eight graduated stitches at the ends which meet to form a mitered corner. When the figures are completed lay in the lines of cross stitches.

This finishes the skeleton or foundation of the motif which, when repeated three times to form the design, will leave a large square space in the centre to be framed with a double line of diagonal kloster blocks just inside the cross stitches and a large triangular space at the centre of each side to be bordered in the same fashion on the two inner edges. In the remaining small square and triangular spaces work small kloster stitch figures.

The threads in the spaces enclosed by the double diagonal kloster blocks should now be cut and drawn, leaving groups of four threads to be woven into bars, those in the centre being decorated with lace stitches (Fig. 13) and those on the sides with twisted diagonal bars (Fig. 15), caught at the centre of each space.

Although the variation of the filling stitches in the openwork spaces is very pleasing, one stitch only might be used and in this case the effect would be even more as if the embroidered fabric had been placed over a lacy background. The crossed diagonal twisted threads such as used to fill the triangular figures on the sides of the embroidered square pictured on page 24 would make a particularly pretty filling for such an effect as this.

Centrepiece with Wrapped Bars

FOR this pretty little centrepiece, which measures seventeen inches square when finished, will be required a piece of Congress canvas about twenty-four inches square counting about twenty-four threads to the inch.

It is unique in having a background of wrapped bars against which the simple geometric pattern stands in strong relief, and in the manner of joining the kloster stitch blocks, which border the different parts of the design, all of the outer points being brought to a mitered corner and a long stitch taken over the joining at the corner (Detail H).

A hem two and one-half inches wide is turned from one corner along two sides and fastened by a band of kloster stitches, over four threads. Then, beginning at the hemmed corner, the figures of the design are outlined with lines and blocks of kloster stitch, taken over four threads of the cloth. It is an easy matter to count this pattern, as there are four threads left in each instance between the corner and side sections of the large repeating motifs. Four threads are also left between the corners of the adjacent motifs at the centre of each side and these threads covered with a straight band of kloster stitch. Detail I shows the way the straight bands of kloster stitch intersect in the centre of the design.

In working the square, begin at the corner and work the solid block, taking the first stitch over two threads, the

second over four threads, and increasing in this way until the ninth and middle stitch covers eighteen threads, then decrease to a point again, and work the double row of half-squares between the corner blocks, there being eight stitches in each half-square.

When all of this work is completed, the other two sides of the cloth are to be hemmed, and the threads cut and drawn for the open part of the design. Four threads are cut and drawn, and four left. These remaining threads are then closely and smoothly wound, using linen thread for the purpose. This makes a pleasing change from the usual style of woven bars, and is rather more quickly executed. The bars may, of course, be woven if preferred.

If a larger cloth is wished, the size may be increased by making it of three or four squares each way, instead of only two as in the model, which would add about six or twelve inches, respectively, to the size of the cloth. As illustrated the design will make a good pillow cover, and may be elongated into an oblong shape by adding two more squares.

Detail H. Corner Section of Centrepiece on Page 26

Detail I. Centre of Centrepiece on Page 26

An All-Over Pattern for Cushions and Bags

Illustration on page 32

THIS pattern will make an effective openwork texture for a pillow top by extending it on all sides, or a double row of blocks, as pictured, running lengthwise the page, will make a good end border for a runner.

The long row of kloster stitches which forms each side of the square open figure consists of forty-one stitches over four threads. The small squares which connect the large ones have thirteen stitches on each side. Outside this figure and worked into the same row of meshes as the kloster stitches are two square eyelets on each side, each one worked over six threads. Between the pairs of eyelets comes a satin stitch figure consisting of ten kloster stitches over four threads then increasing to six, eight, ten, twelve, and back to six again for the diamond-shaped centre, then ten more stitches over four threads to finish.

In cutting the threads for the open centres of the large square figures notice that eight threads are cut in the centre of each side, leaving two groups of four threads on each side of the corner. After these threads have been woven into bars lay the threads through the centre of the wide space and weave a "spider" in the centre.

The small squares are filled with woven and twisted bars as illustrated in Fig. 15.

This pattern is especially effective when worked in white mercerized cotton on an écru ground — a pleasing combination for all articles for use in the living room.

Centrepiece in All-Over Design

WHEN worked upon fine material this pattern is very delicate and lacy. Eighty-eight threads must be allowed for each block. If your material counts about twenty-eight threads to the inch the centrepiece pictured will finish about sixteen inches square. Worked upon a coarser canvas or on scrim the size would be considerably increased. It can easily be made into a square with straight edges by omitting the four outer squares at each corner.

The canvas is first divided into squares having twelve diagonal kloster blocks on each side. Three patterns are used for filling in these squares, and are so used that no

two of the same pattern come side by side. For one pattern the fabric threads enclosed by the diagonal kloster blocks are cut and drawn in both directions in groups of four in the usual way, leaving four threads which are woven into bars with lace stitch filling (Fig. 13) in all except the outer spaces.

Another pattern leaves a small canvas square counting six diagonal blocks each way in the centre of the larger square. Upon this little enclosed square a cross is worked with arms extending to the middle of each side of the square (Detail J). This cross is started at the centre mesh of the canvas square with four stitches

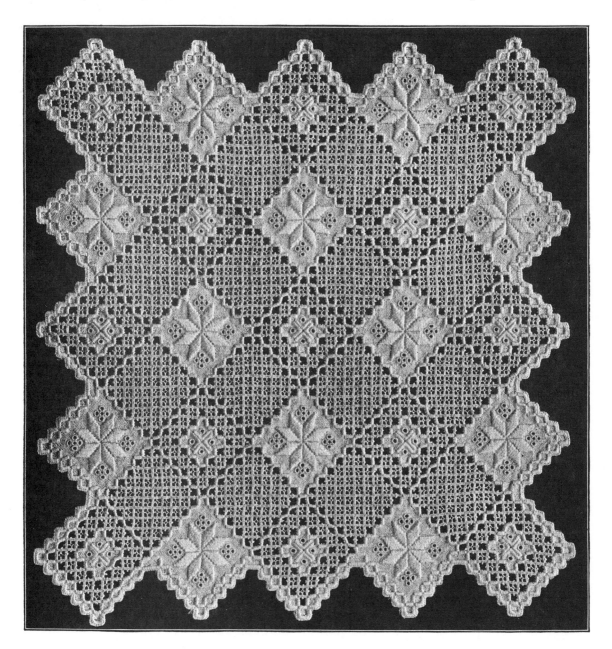

each taken from the centre mesh over four threads, perpendicularly and horizontally. In the triangular spaces between these stitches the four arms are worked, each arm consisting of two rows of six stitches over four placed diagonally to each other but meeting in the same mesh. A single eyelet is worked in each space between the arms. Around this central figure the threads are drawn and woven into picoted bars, and the middle row of spaces filled with lace stitch. Detail A shows the work in process.

For the third pattern an eight-pointed star is worked in the centre of a canvas space, each of the sections being increased by twos for twelve stitches, and then decreased in the same way. Groups of eyelets are worked in each of the four corners (Detail K).

The edge is the usual

Detail K. Eight-pointed Star in Process

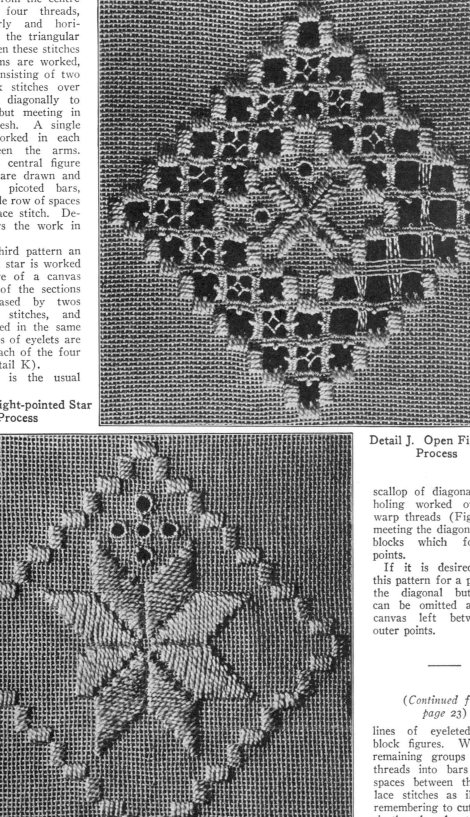

Detail J. Open Figure in Process

scallop of diagonal buttonholing worked over four warp threads (Fig. 9) and meeting the diagonal kloster blocks which form the points.

If it is desired to use this pattern for a pillow top the diagonal buttonholing can be omitted and plain canvas left between the outer points.

———

(Continued from page 23)

lines of eyeleted kloster block figures. Weave the remaining groups of four threads into bars and fill spaces between them with lace stitches as illustrated, remembering to cut the fabric threads only at the ends of the stitches forming the kloster blocks and not along the sides.

An Adaptable Design

FIND the exact centre of your cloth, which should be 250 threads from the edge each way, and around a centre square of twelve threads work two kloster stitch blocks on each side separated by four threads, the end stitches of the blocks meeting at the corners being taken into the same mesh. Outside of these blocks work a triangular figure on each side. Starting three threads to the right of the small kloster block and in the same row of meshes with the top of this block, work four stitches over four threads, four over eight, five over twelve, four over eight, and four over four. At right angles to this work the next figure and so on around the square (see Detail L). Next come two rows of double back stitch taken diagonally over two threads, and then the long bars of kloster stitch taken over four threads and separated by four threads, each bar thirty-seven stitches in length and joined to the adjacent bar at the ends by a kloster block (five stitches over four threads). Close to the ends of these bars comes a double row of diagonal kloster blocks which finishes the figure. Framing this centre motif and separated from it by twelve threads, comes a straight border with ornamental corners. Work first the thirteen kloster block figures on each side (Detail L) and the twelve diagonal blocks connecting them across the corners (Detail M), next the straight band of kloster stitch forming the base of the kloster block figures on the sides and meeting at the corners. Leave twelve threads,

work a second row of straight parallel stitches over four threads, and in the space between them work a row of graduated stitches over two, four, and six threads as shown in Detail M, which is also a detail of the corner motif.

The wide border is a repetition of the centre motif. First lay the diagonal blocks which extend from the outer straight band and form the inner edge of this line of repeating motifs, next the straight lines and connecting blocks which form the outer border and in the square spaces which remain work the four-sided figures. There should be four canvas threads between the tips of the points formed by the diagonal blocks and the topmost block between the solid vertical lines of stitches in the outer border. If preferred this outer border can be started by working a line of diagonal blocks on the two outer sides of the space to be left for the square figures and the solid lines of stitchery worked from each alternate block. There should be thirty-seven parallel stitches in each solid line as in the centre motif.

Not until all of this solid work has been done should the fabric threads be cut and drawn for the open portions of the design, and the various fancy filling stitches put in.

A close examination of the details will show that the stitch which looks so much like brier stitch is not that familiar embroidery stitch, but a canvas stitch worked from the bottom of a space toward the top, each time picking up two canvas threads on the diagonal, keeping the working thread alternately to the right and left of the needle in succeeding stitches so that it does not cross itself. This stitch should be done with the same size thread as used for the solid parts of the design.

Alternating with this stitch is another which also works upward. Make the vertical stitch first, then the

(Above) **Detail L**
(Left) **Detail M**

diagonal stitch to right and left, each one taken over four canvas threads and placed as shown in the details, which are very nearly actual size.

This is an unusually adaptable design. The outer border only might be used and extended as much as desired. If a cloth with a hemmed edge is wanted the inner border with triangular corner motifs can be used, omitting the central motif if desired.

All-Over Design for Bags or Cushions
Description on page 27